Why do I feel like this?

A simple explanation of why you feel the way you do and how to improve it

Kelley Waters

Dedication

For Dom, Ben and G, such superb humans.

Foreword

I first met Kelley after she had just graduated from the European School of Osteopathy in 1999. She was highly recommended to me as a promising young osteopath and turned out to be an excellent locum for my London practice. We became firm friends.

Kelley is a highly respected and knowledgeable practitioner who knows the importance of empowering her patients. She helps them understand *why* they feel the way they do, explaining how we work as humans and the problems our bodies and souls endure, in a way that makes this valuable information accessible and clear.

There are many publications on this topic but very few that encapsulate it in such a reachable way. This book is a comforting and helpful read in a difficult ever-changing and evolving world.

Timothy D H John

D.O., F.S.C.C.O.

Registered Osteopath

Contents

Why do I feel like this?

Modern life can be challenging and leave you feeling jaded and inadequate. But what if instead of being defective or damaged you are simply a human being covered in layers of adaptive coping?

We are expected to be human without really understanding what it means to be human. It's like we've been given a supercar to drive with no driving lessons or licence. We are speeding around trying to navigate the road, the obstacles, the gear changes, feeling out of control at times and at the mercy of every bump and bend.

This book will help you start to put the pieces of your human puzzle together. It's a simple explanation of why you make sense, alongside tips to help you better balance your wellness dials and signposts to further information. It will leave you feeling that you are driving the car and not that the car is driving you, moving you from survival mode to thriving mode.

In it, I break down your primal survival settings and brain and body chemistry, how these may be being negatively manipulated in the modern world and what you can do to take charge and feel better.

"I've learned how to be in the present."

"How?" asked the boy.

"I find a quiet spot and shut my eyes and breathe."

Charlie Mackesy

Introduction

"The ancients knew something that we seem to have forgotten."

Albert Einstein

The world has dramatically changed in the hundreds of thousands of years we humans have walked the planet, but *we* haven't changed much at all. Our basic way of dealing with life remains pretty much as it was for our early ancestors: we want to avoid danger and feel safe and needed.

We're all dealing with a lot and there is no magic pill to take the hardships away. This book is a realistic look at how to cope better and take back some control of your reactions and responses to the circumstances in which you find yourself.

Over my years in practice, I have noticed it helps my patients when I explain the basics around their human design; their physical and mental symptoms make a lot more sense when they understand how their system works.

Most of us were taught to calculate Pythagoras' theorem and critique Shakespeare at school (and these can be extremely worthwhile skills), but the average education did not teach us how to understand and cope with being a human.

In my work as an osteopath, I focus on the entire body, not just the part that hurts. To an osteopath, every part of you is interconnected and if one part isn't working properly, it can affect your overall health.

The founder of osteopathy was a man called Andrew Taylor Still and for him it was a *belief system.* Still was awed by the natural self-regulating tendency of the human machine and based his system of treatment on the principle that if you pointed the body in the right direction, it would, in most cases, heal itself.

This principle holds as strong today as it did in the late 1800s: given half the chance, your human body is always leaning towards repair and harmony.

A thorough knowledge of anatomy (what's there) and physiology (how it works) means the osteopath can, for example, trace your headaches back to that ankle injury you sustained two years ago (the effects that short-term limping had on the leg muscles, how it altered the mechanics of your hips and pelvis and caused your spine and shoulders to adapt and compensate, resulting in your neck muscles pulling on their insertion point at the back of your head and hey bingo! You've got a headache).

Osteopaths work alongside a naturally occurring process in the body called homeostasis. This is your body's internal thermostat, working to keep things stable and balanced, thus allowing your body to maintain a steady state despite changes in the environment or your activities.

Imagine it as a tightrope walker constantly adjusting to stay centred. Your body is always striving to keep things just right, like maintaining a consistent temperature, blood pressure, and pH level. When things get out of balance, like when you're too hot or too cold, or your blood sugar levels are too high or too low, your body kicks into gear to bring things back to normal.

This balancing act is essential for your health and survival, ensuring that your body's systems can work properly and efficiently. When you come to see me for treatment, be it for osteopathy or coaching, my job isn't to fix you. My job is to tap into your body's healing mechanisms and your mind's ability to self-reflect. Above all my job is to give you greater understanding and a sense of hope — you can feel better.

I learnt early on in my career as a newly qualified, slightly overwhelmed osteopath that if I took all the responsibility (including the praise and acclaim) for someone getting better, it was going to be a rocky journey. This was going to need to be a partnership — between the patient's afore-mentioned homeostatic capacity and my skills.

A lot of the time, we feel that our bodies are against us. We try to figure out what is *wrong* and forget that our bodies are on our side and our minds are simply playing out the thoughts they have been programmed with.

It is helpful to observe how your own mind and body get by and what tactics you employ to survive *your* world. How are the universal primal survival traits showing up in your day-to-day life?

I have heard many stories and treated many wonderful patients over my years in practice and I feel blessed to have learnt a great deal from them all. In my experience, what most patients seek are two things:

- **a simple explanation of what's happening to them** and
- **to feel better**

If you have picked up this book, you probably want the same.

So much self-help is focused on 'finding and fixing yourself'. But before you can understand *who* you are, it helps to understand *what* you are and *why* you do the things you do. Perhaps it isn't so much that something is *wrong* with you but that you are just being human.

We can all benefit from understanding how our clever minds and bodies work. In the following chapters, I've incorporated the human themes that show up with patients, and towards the end, I give simple tools to turn your wellness dials in the right direction.

In a treatment session I want to know what's troubling you, but I also want to understand what the story is behind your problem and what else might have contributed to it — the precipitating and maintaining factors. I'll ask you appropriate medical screening questions, what your life is made up of and build a picture of who you are *behind* your symptoms.

If you tell me your back 'went' the same week that you had an argument with your boss, your child left for university, and you had to lift your elderly parent into bed, we start to build context around your pain: your system was already in brace-brace mode, and the lifting was the final straw pushing your tense muscles and joints to stretch too far.

As your case history develops, I'll explain the basics of how your body and mind work — the link between the two and how past experiences and injuries may *still* be influencing you years on.

We'll discuss that you are wired for survival and can become 'full up' with mental and physical stress until it overflows into your system and shows as pain, dysfunction, a state of languish, or illness. We'll talk about your body's chemistry and how its balance is being disturbed by modern life.

During treatment or coaching we work together as detectives investigating your story, making sense of it, and looking for opportunities to make positive and realistic changes.

We might notice any unhelpful thought themes

that are hampering your wellness and as the process continues a sense of optimism emerges because self-knowledge is fuel for positive change.

Our clever design served our ancestors well and it can do the same for us if we play to its strengths.

Remember, you are a fabulous creation capable of amazing things, you make sense, and you most certainly *can* feel better.

Once you understand the basics of how your mind and body are responding to the life you are leading you are already making steps in a better direction.

1

Your human operating system

"To know thyself is the beginning of wisdom."

Socrates

So, what *are* you?

You are the owner of a mind and a body.

We'll call the mind and body bit your 'human operating system'. It has survived and thrived on our planet for a long, long while.

You are made a certain way for you to have the best chances of survival. This means you will:

- strive to do what needs to be done
- sense danger and assess risk
- respond mentally and physically to this danger and
- reset and recover from physical and emotional trauma

To achieve the above, you have a set of primal tools that you employ (mostly unconsciously) as you go about your life.

Becoming aware of these primal tools at play will help you to cope better with what life throws at you. As you read on you will see that any mental and physical pain you are suffering makes more sense in the context of your human design.

Human 'being' is indeed a complex juggle. Your clever human operating system must constantly respond to the sensory overload, repetitive minor, and unprocessed major stresses it is bombarded with, and this means, from time to time, glitches show up. As Glennon Doyle (ref 1) said, "It's not hard because you are getting it wrong, it is hard because it is hard".

I have treated thousands of patients with problems ranging from headaches to heartache. We discuss how their bodies feel and what's on their minds. When I listen to their physical symptoms and mental worries, what I hear is their human operating system explaining their wellness level.

When things are tough that level could be a 1/10. My aim in the treatment room and in writing this book is to significantly raise the score for them and for you. Whatever has happened to you in your life will be held in your system and as Bessel Van Der Kolk (ref 2) says, your body literally *keeps the score.*

During a session we talk about the symptoms a patient presents with and so much more. We chat about family, relationships, work, and the *juggle.* We discuss the planet and what is in the news, and whether we should watch it. We talk about magic and mortality and what happens when someone dies. How grief is *all the love we now can't give.*

We talk about beloved pets and the state of the potholes on our roads. We speak about recipes, the joy and monotony of cooking, gardening, and the feeling of feet in sand. We talk about books and book clubs, bee keeping and fishing, and the changing of seasons.

We chat about divorce and education, privilege and hardship, and how both can coexist. The black, the white, the grey, the yin, and the yang. We talk about silver linings and seasonal affected disorder (SAD), puberty, menopause, partners, parenting and how you are only as happy as your *least* happy child.

We discuss *not* having babies and adopting. We ruminate on being the jam in the sandwich between two generations and the reality of caring for ageing parents whilst clinging to the notion that there is still someone more grown up than us in life.

We discuss regrets and fears, hopes and dreams. Most of all we share the vulnerable, all-encompassing experience of being a human. In every session and behind every case I treat is the story of a person trying their best to cope with the life they are leading.

Their physical symptoms reflect injuries and the stress response showing up in their body alongside the side effects of mental survival strategies and beliefs (most likely developed in early years) that may no longer be working especially well.

Who they were before life got hold of them will

still be sitting there under these accumulated layers. When we better understand our human design the puzzle pieces start to fall into place.

You are not broken or damaged but laden with adaptations and compensations. You are a juggling act of stress doses, thresholds, and well-trodden responses which are often triggering past symptoms and injuries. It is in identifying these physical and mental coping strategies and their side effects that you can start to see the wood from the trees.

The answer to most problems, be they physical or mental, is to seek a different perspective and find context. Even in life-threatening situations where you are struggling with serious illness or trauma, it is empowering to regain a semblance of control and not feel entirely at the mercy of life. That is what treatment and self-reflection are all about: a different view of your history, your pain, and the story you are telling yourself. Perspective is a very useful tool.

When we look at ourselves through this wider, more compassionate lens, we can get clarity and from this comes a sense of hope. It's as if we take steps back from the painting until we can see the picture more clearly. What this wider perspective also unveils is 'frame of reference'. It helps us understand not only what drives our own behaviour but also what drives those around us.

As the practitioner, I have the privilege of having a bird's eye view of you, and from this vantage point, I can help you take *everything* into consideration.

You are very well-designed, but you have probably been pushed a bit too hard. In this book I am going to show you what themes I incorporate when I work with patients so that you can make some sense of and improve how *you* feel.

There are great books, podcasts, TED talks and research studies which explain the following concepts in further detail, and I will refer to their authors in references and further reading. They are pioneers in their field and are also my heroes. I would highly recommend you look them up.

The bad news is that being human can be hard. The good news is that this book will help you to feel better in yourself.

2

You're only human

"What we don't need in the midst of struggle is shame for being human."

Brené Brown

You're only human, but you're very special! As far as nature is concerned you are a highly successful creature — but you haven't evolved much (or at least human beings haven't evolved much) over time. Unlike the iPhone (which at the time of writing is currently on model 16 and running iOS 18), the human operating system hasn't had much of an update, and you could argue it hasn't needed to. After all it has survived and thrived for a long, long while.

Your brain may have developed to include more areas of higher function (which differentiates you from other animals), but it hasn't let go of the parts that protect you and promote your survival. These areas, such as the hypervigilant amygdala, are as engaged in you today as they were hundreds of thousands of years ago in your ancestors.

You are still operating from the original software package that enabled those ancestors to have the best chance of survival — namely an ability to sense and respond to danger, a drive towards safety in numbers and a self-repairing mechanism.

This required you to watch out for and respond to threats, communicate effectively with your people, and respect your body's needs. The rules of good mental and physical health haven't changed, but our environment has.

For us humans, glitches occur when either repetitive or unresolved stress triggers clog and overwhelm the system and it doesn't have time to rest and repair. It's like you have too many tabs open — a game of whack-a-mole that you are losing. Our world is now, more than ever, geared towards overstimulation, with psychological prompts triggering us to click the next link, scroll on, or stay constantly connected. Without any other pressures (unlikely) this is enough to leave us feeling jaded.

A huge part of the (billion dollar) self-help industry is based on the concept that somewhere in the future is a place where you can be fixed — a kind of heaven on earth where you update your system and emerge as a better, happier, more successful human.

The marketing message here is that by finding the magic elixir, your shortcomings and difficulties will be erased and you will become the *mended* version of yourself. The *false* premise, of course, is that you need fixing and that somewhere outside of yourself is the solution where there will be light and not darkness, happiness not sadness, joy not pain.

Contrast, however, is part of the natural world and is fundamental to life. Light doesn't exist without dark — we can't work out what we like if there isn't anything to dislike.

We spend a lot of our time in physical discomfort, feeling a bit weird and a bit fearful. We know our mind's thoughts intimately, but we only know other people from what they choose to show us. What I have learnt in all my years in practice is that there is not a single person who isn't in some way suffering from the *human condition.*

By better understanding our design and the challenges it faces in our current environment, we can set ourselves free from the feeling of being broken or weak and realise we are incredible creatures trying to navigate the modern world with our original biological, physical, and psychological operating systems.

As much as you don't wish ill on anyone, you do feel better when someone says, "me too". You're not being mean by the way — you're just human and you don't want to be different.

We like to feel we are not the only ones, that we are not alone. It reduces our shame, and shame is something we could all do without. We don't like to be the odd ones out and we really like to fit in, even if it's only with an image of what we believe we should be.

Your human operating system works in a feedback loop. It's wired to react to stimuli. What your mind senses, your body responds to and vice versa. What I see in practice in patients' presenting symptoms are often the effects of this system at play in modern life.

Your human self was designed to stick by a **set of rules** to keep safe. Imagine Mother Nature on your shoulder whispering in your ear:

stay in the gang — know and be known by your tribe. Be the same as the others and fit in!

know your place — be needed, hierarchy matters, don't step out of line!

confirmation bias — look for evidence that you are right! Your brain notices mostly what you are looking for!

negativity bias — assume the worst, it's best to worry and constantly risk-assess!

repetition and familiarity bias — stick to what you know and don't eat those strange berries!

stay vigilant — be alert and watch out for danger! Use fight, flight, fawn or freeze to get out of trouble!

These rules were very useful and worked wonders back in the day, but they may be causing a few issues now as you use them in your modern life. Being aware of their influence as you navigate your day-to-day existence is essential so that you are the master not the slave.

How we feel is also largely dependent on our chemistry. Serotonin, dopamine, endorphins and oxytocin are four of many important chemicals which when in relative balance enhance our sense of wellbeing. Serotonin is our mood and energy level enhancer and is released by us nourishing our body. Dopamine is released as a reward for effort and is linked to motivation. It gives us the desire to do what we need to do and increases when we get a task done. Endorphins help us cope with psychological and physical stress and are released through physical activity and exertion, and oxytocin bonds us to each other, promoting positive feelings and is released through connection. The balance of these chemical ingredients can be negatively influenced by our modern world if we don't stay aware and in charge of it.

Your body and mind need these wellbeing cocktail ingredients and will drive and push to get them, come what may. Modern life and technology offer unhealthy shortcuts, so you need to be aware of them so that you can be more in charge and less manipulated. As neuroscientist Andrew Huberman (ref 3) says, "addiction is the gradual narrowing of what brings you pleasure, and a good life is the gradual expansion of what brings you pleasure".

Imagine you start every day with a jug of dopamine at your disposal waiting to be released after you make an effort. Remember the dopamine reward is nature's way of ensuring you get the important stuff done and is part of your ancestral survival plan.

Unfortunately, the technology industry knows this, which is why app developers create features such as face identity recognition, reducing barriers to entry. If you look at your phone screen you are 'back into' the phone. Their next job is to make sure you stay there as long as possible.

First thing in the morning, making your bed, emptying the dishwasher and getting other jobs done before you go off to work sets you up for the day with a sense of achievement and a dopamine reward for completing tasks. If instead you scroll through your phone (bouncing from your alarm snooze to your email, WhatsApp and a quick (5-10-minute) scroll of dopamine-flooding Instagram) you release a quick hit of dopamine with little effort. When you eventually get to your desk and do the hard stuff that would healthily release your dopamine reserve, there won't be much left. This means you won't feel pleasure when you complete that difficult task - it doesn't get rewarded and so won't get reinforced, leading to an increase in future procrastination and reduced overall motivation. Putting off that first phone dive for an hour after you wake will set a far better tone for the rest of your day as you'll have reserves of wellbeing ingredients in your pantry.

How you feel is heavily influenced by how your primal survival settings and chemistry are being manipulated. Understanding this makes sense of some of the mental and physical symptoms you suffer from time to time. You're just human and it's not just you. We're all fighting the challenge of over-and under-stimulation, and we all feel strange and wonky at times.

3

What's your story?

"Human beings have an innate need to bond and connect."

Johann Hari

Humans are social creatures who gather to feel safe. We've always been drawn to grouping together and the campfire provided us with a place to heal, bond, and relate through the sharing of experiences and stories. We needed and still need to be *connected* to our tribe.

We have a strong drive for intimacy. After food and shelter there is an instinctive need to matter, which shows that you are relied upon, valued, and loved. To have social proof that you belong is essential to your wellbeing. Recent studies on the catastrophic effects of loneliness on health are testimony to this.

As well as telling others your stories, you also tell them to yourself to cope with your experiences — you distort, delete, and generalise facts to fit your version of events. From early childhood, you start to write this narrative (and pages are added from external sources) that essentially forms the basis of your beliefs about you and your world. The data you have collected and the tapestry you then weave out of it becomes your reality.

Your subconscious mind's job is to create your autobiography from your programming, and your world is an expression of how you are using and have used your mind and body.

It is helpful to regularly check whether all the parts of your narrative hold truth. If you go through life without questioning your thoughts, you suffer far more than you need to. Dare to be wrong and literally change your mind.

Your stories (which can contribute to your mental and physical pain) may well be false and yet you are creating your life from them. By reframing and changing the running commentary in your head, you can change the belief you hold about yourself (your identity) and improve how you feel. Likewise, by improving your physical state you can change your mental outlook.

Some situations are extremely difficult and have no immediate solution, but telling your story — reviewing, understanding, and where appropriate reframing it, is therapeutic. This is demonstrated by how much patients talk about their lives in treatment sessions even when they appear to be coming in with purely physical symptoms. They benefit from reflecting on their thoughts and feelings.

Physical symptoms are also often better treated and understood in this context as the body's defensive barriers drop, allowing treatment to have greater effect.

Comparison is often the thief of joy in our modern world, but back in your hunter-gatherer days it was a useful survival tool which helped you know your place in the tribe. As a hunter-gatherer, your tribe would have comprised of approximately 50 to 100 members. That was the number of people you would have been comparing yourself to, and in a relationship with over, your lifetime and it was manageable.

Nowadays due to the wonders of modern technology you can scroll on your phone whilst you sit in a waiting room and compare yourself to hundreds of people through a device that enables you to see the perfectly curated image of someone on the other side of the planet.

Add to this the measurable 'likes' you receive on social media (which play to your ancient primal desire for approval) and is it any wonder you can feel inadequate as you navigate your technology-dominated world? Ten minutes of random scrolling on your phone can result in fifty separate images telling you that your life is not as good as theirs.

You are essentially comparing your raw inner self to somebody else's polished outer self and it's helpful to remember that as far as social media goes you are not the customer but the product.

As Edward Tufte (ref 4) says, "there are only two industries that call their customers 'users' – illegal drugs and software".

Many tech experts are now warning of the dangers of unregulated screen time. Tristan Harris, former Google Design Ethicist and Co-founder and President of the Center for Humane

Technology, (ref 5) says, "social media wants things from you. We have moved from having a tools-based technology environment to a manipulation and addiction-based technology environment. Social media isn't a tool that is waiting to be used. It has its own goals and means of pursuing them by manipulating our psychology".

This is not to demonise advances in technology. A great deal of good can also come from it and, let's face it, it's here to stay. My point is that we are all at risk of being zombified by it if we a) don't understand its effects and b) don't stay vigilant of them.

The underlying message that you are not enough or do not have enough is powerful and pervasive. Amidst the relentless bombardment of instantly available products that promise to bolster this sense of self-lack and dissociation is the message that you need something or someone outside of yourself to be complete. Remember your brain is wired to keep you safe and alive. If it perceives you are somehow falling short or are inadequate (and therefore of no use to your tribe), alarms will begin to sound in the system.

Status is very important to us humans — you don't want to be rejected by your people and eaten by that tiger, now do you? We sometimes feel a sense of inadequacy and imposter syndrome, which is in part driven by this comparison wiring. Understanding this primal tendency helps us to notice when it is being overstimulated and avoid triggers when and where we can.

We are programmed to react to anything our system perceives as a threat and most of our behaviour comes from our subconscious coding and primal instincts. This makes sense of some of the 'human' struggles we have.

4

That voice in your head

"Whether you think you can or think you can't, you're right."

Henry Ford

Another universal feature of us humans is the narrative that runs in our heads. It's a huge relief to my patients when they realise that *they are not their thoughts.*

Think of that self-talk as a running commentary, your monkey mind or a script that you collate over your lifetime. This chatter builds the basis of your feelings, beliefs, identity, and behaviour and left unchecked can wreak havoc.

This script is often the loudest voice in your head and starts early on, but sadly no one teaches us about it in school. In fact, many of our script voices are created and reinforced during our education as we struggle to process a history lesson when the voice in our head tells us we are not good enough or are stupid. Being in brace-brace mode whilst trying to memorise the Battle of Hastings doesn't tend to go so well.

There's a good reason why we worry. One thing our human brain detests is the unknown. We like to make sense of things and find answers. Worrying makes something frightening and uncertain slightly more certain. Even if the worry thought is negative, it will trigger a little rewarding shot of dopamine, so worrying and ruminating becomes a habit.

We like to attach thoughts to the emotions we are feeling, which means we move into our conscious minds and don't allow the emotion or feeling to process and pass. It gets stuck in the system.

I learnt about 'the script' voice from Richard Wilkins (ref 6) and Liz Ivory (ref 7), who are experts in this field and run transformative courses on it.

The voice or script never tells you everything is 'just as it should be' and that you can 'rest at ease'. It is there to keep you under control and make sure you don't venture far from safety. The message is that it is better to play small and keep your head down so that you are safe in your tribe.

This was effective back when you were a hunter-gatherer and may have felt necessary when you were a child, but it now comes with hefty side effects. In fact, the voice in our head and the story it concocts can be at the root of most of our problems. Our bodies are always listening to our thoughts and reflecting our mood, as is demonstrated by the recognisable 'postures' of depressed people or teenagers.

We are born with brains that are primed for programming. As young children up until age seven, we are essentially walking around with the record button on. This is like being under a state of semi-hypnosis, which enables us to learn how to be human as we download the programmes we are surrounded by.

When I work with patients on their narratives,

and we list some of their inner thoughts they can easily summon up their repetitive script voice statements such as:

"I'm not good enough",

"I'm too much",

"I don't fit in", and

"Bad things always happen to me".

Yet when we discuss positive statements about them, such as:

"I am creative", and

"I am a loyal friend",

they will come up with many reasons why these aren't true despite clear evidence to the contrary. That pesky negative bias is at play again!

The voice in your head and the resultant story you tell yourself are extremely influential. Most importantly your mind will tell you barefaced lies. It helps to know that the negative voice or script will usually talk in sentences such as "I'm not clever enough", whereas your true voice will talk to you in terms of "yes", "no", "stop", "not that" or "enough". The most important conversation you ever have is with yourself because thinking leads to actions, which leads to results. As much of our behaviour comes from our preprogrammed subconscious, it is worth questioning whether you are living the life you want to live or the life you've been coded to live. This is why separating you from your inner voice or script is vital.

The job of any therapist is to play *you* back to *you*. Self-reflection is the first step to feeling better and if we can approach what we find difficult about ourselves with curiosity and not shame we can see the bigger picture. This naturally leads to self-compassion and clarity, unearthing you from the heavy weight of that negative pixie that sits on your shoulder.

Your thoughts powerfully determine outcomes and heavily influence your sense of self-agency (your belief in your ability to achieve goals and overcome challenges), so it helps to be aware of this and pay close attention to what your own running commentary is. We are all aware of how two people can perceive and recall the same situation differently. We are heavily influenced by our preconceptions.

Be conscious of what thought ingredients and actions you are putting into your day. Mindset drives behaviour, which drives actions, and actions drive outcomes. As Tom Palmer (ref 8) says, "Pessimism is self-fulfilling". It might sound obvious, but if you want to have a good outcome, be optimistic and do the best you can.

A simple rule is to ask yourself if you would choose to think what you are thinking. Would you choose to run the thought, "I always mess things up"?

If the answer is no, then as the aforementioned Richard and Liz say, you are not choosing, something else is. I'll bet it's the well-practised voice in your head which developed in childhood when you needed to make sense of what was happening to you. It will have been reinforced by primal survival instincts, family, friends, culture, the media and much more. If you have spent your life telling yourself or surrounded by people telling you that you're not good enough, you will most likely believe it.

This is why you can be disappointed when you change your external environment (move house, change partner, change job) in the hope you will *feel* better. As Jon Kabat-Zinn (ref 9) said, "Wherever you go, there you are".

That voice in your head is not you but it will loyally follow you. You are *not* your thoughts, so don't believe everything that you think. The greatest mental liberation comes from recognising your internal running commentary as part of your primal human survival makeup and identifying it as such. That way you can see it more for what it is: a meddling lifetime script and not your actual truth.

You can *choose* to think differently.

A key tool for feeling better is to identify the running script in your head and learn to separate from it.

5

Anxiety and pain

"Anxiety does not empty tomorrow of its sorrows but only empties today of its strength."

Charles Spurgeon

This may sound strange, but anxiety is normal. You are meant to feel anxious at times. We tend to believe this is some kind of illness or system failure when in fact it is a normal human alarm response to uncertainty or threat in our environment.

The same goes for pain, which is often a message from the body that it is compromised (and that message could be that you have been sitting hunched over a screen for too long or put your hand on the hot hob) or that the pathway from a previous injury has become too well-trodden and easily triggered long after the original insult has healed.

Anxiety is an effective survival tool. It is a sign of a raised alarm state in the body, which your mind is trying to make sense of and it can be very disturbing and difficult to cope with. The system goes into brace-brace mode as it would on a turbulent flight.

This age-old body response was designed to ensure you lived: if you 'felt' alarm or pain, you paid keen attention and therefore had a better chance of survival.

In the wild it was better to be the person who assumed the snapping twig sound was a predator and not just a rabbit. Mother Nature didn't design you to be footloose and fancy-free — she gave you a hefty dose of *negativity bias* and we humans alive today are the descendants of the gene pool of folk who took their medicine.

This of course leads us to focus more on what could go *wrong* than what could go *right*! The stress response in your body is your way of reacting to perceived threats and limiting their impact — your system gears up with an increase in, for example, heart rate, muscle tension, and breathing.

The effects of stress result in your blood supply being redirected away from the higher functioning centres of the brain to the areas that coordinate survival. This is because you don't need to waste precious resources doing algebra and instead need to focus on staying alive. It's like you go into limp-home mode.

This is why it is harder to think creatively, show emotional flexibility and regulate your emotions when you are stressed. Your brain has diverted resources away from these more evolved areas and into the vital ones.

Once the threat has passed, the counterbalance to your stress response is mediated by the rest and digest side of your nervous system — to slow things down and reset you. We don't have direct control over our automatic nervous system in the way we do over our movement or voice, but we can heavily influence it and we will discuss how in chapter 9 when we look at wellness tools.

When you are anxious, your human operating system is just doing what it is programmed to do. Problems occur when this natural alarm state persists and becomes an obstacle to everyday life — when we continue in brace-brace position long after the plane has landed.

When you are in pain, having a panic attack, or in an anxious state — or just feeling overwhelmed — you have moved along the scale from being able to use your thinking brain rationally into a state of unease and hypersensitivity.

This sense of alarm or pain can even happen when there *isn't* anything wrong in that precise moment, which further enhances the problem as you are left feeling you are crazy to feel so disproportionately anxious or sore. Your stress and pain smoke alarms have become so sensitised that they are triggered by a match being lit.

It is as if your body and mind are operating from an emergency memo. This is a normal response to stress triggers — if you were being chased by that tiger in the wild, you would immediately stop trying to wistfully count the stars and what's more, if you survived, you would always listen out for future tigers.

The best thing to do to help yourself when you have long-term (chronic) pain or anxiety is to attend to your body's overactive, sensitised state. You can't be talked out of anxiety; you need to first calm your body's alarm systems.

This is why going back to basics is often the best first aid treatment. You need to give your human operating system a healing medicinal concoction of rest, warmth, breathing, nourishment, connection, distraction, nature, and movement with a spoonful of reassurance and self-compassion to help the medicine go down. After this, your sensory system will begin to assess your environment more accurately and not see tigers at every turn.

In some cases, prescribed or over-the-counter drugs can serve to calm the anxiety or pain and bridge the gap until the root cause can be addressed. Pain relief can help to give your body a rest from the over-trodden nerve pathways and give your brain a chance to consider other pain-free routes and reset. For a percentage of people, medication remains a more permanent tool in their toolbox.

Talking therapy can be extremely helpful in addressing what may have precipitated the episode and help build context and future coping strategies. Reprogramming your mind's association with an old pain pathway by, for example, smiling as you get up from a chair rather than wincing, has been shown in studies (and seen in my patients) to dramatically lower pain levels over time.

I would highly recommend the work of Dr Russell Kennedy (see the Further Reading section) who has created an approach that blends both the art and science of healing from chronic anxiety and worry. He treats the underlying alarm in the system rather than focusing on the negative thoughts alone. His book *Anxiety RX,* podcasts and online course are both accessible and transformational.

Once the acute anxiety response in your human operating system has calmed, you can start to look at the underlying stories and causes behind it and desensitise your smoke alarm.

6

Who is driving the car?

"Our brains are wired for connection, but trauma rewires them for survival."

Ryan North

Messages of scarcity and threat are all around you — there is very rarely anything on the late-night news to tell you all is well in the world, so be mindful of what you watch, read, and hear. As Morgan Housel (ref 10) says, "Read more books so that you can make better sense of the news you do watch ".

Add this scary messaging to your natural tendency towards the previously mentioned *Negative*, *Confirmation* and *Familiarity Bias* and your stress dials can get turned up to maximum.

Sensors in the body will detect a real or perceived threat and gear you for either flight, fight, freeze, or fawn, depending on what is going to give you the best chance of survival. It's important to note that the brain finds it hard to differentiate between something real and something imagined, which is why, for example, a loud noise to a war veteran could trigger a flood of alarm responses, transposing him or her back to the battlefield.

The first of these four trauma responses, **flight,** occurs when our brain perceives that we have a good chance to escape the danger. It's the first and most desirable option because it gets us out of the dangerous situation and into safety with relatively low risk. We move *away* from the challenge.

In our modern world, flight doesn't necessarily look like running from a tiger. It could mean leaving a job or relationship when things get tricky or simply staring out the window and daydreaming to 'leave' the conversation (something children do at school when they might look like they are not listening but are in a stressed state and using the mental flight response to cope).

In some situations, we can't escape, but we have the strength and resources to cope so we **fight** — whether it's verbally by standing up for ourselves when someone reverses their car into ours or physically by picking a fight and attacking others or defending ourselves. This is an aggressive response that moves *towards* the challenge.

When our bodies **freeze**, our brain has determined that fleeing or fighting is not an option. We have an urge to *hide* from the problem. The nervous system has made the decision to play dead because we perceive that there's no way out without making the situation worse and we simply can't deal with it. This could look like not speaking up in a meeting or staying under the duvet on an exam day.

Fawn kicks in when we can't flee, we can't fight, and freezing wouldn't cut it, so instead we try to *befriend* the danger, make ourselves agreeable to the threat and do whatever it takes to appease. This could look like flattering someone to deflect their mood, taking the blame when it isn't your fault or overexplaining yourself. Fawners often use the words "I'm just..." as if to 'justify' their actions.

These stress responses are complex, protective, and essential to our survival and sometimes with hindsight we wish we had chosen a different one! Ultimately, our body picks what it perceives to give us our best chance, but it's important to note that these can become habitual and most likely reflect what we learnt to do as children.

By noticing where we used to go and where we go now in times of stress, we can start to understand how our habitual stress responses are reflected in our behaviour and symptoms. Where does your stress show in your body? What are the warning signals your body gives you that you are becoming overcooked? Does your jaw tighten or the base of your neck prickle? Does the ringing in your ears get louder after three back-to-back meetings? When you finally get that weekend migraine, could your body be really saying, "I tried to tell you"?

Which of the four stress responses do you tend to go to when under pressure? Do you initially fawn and then move on to flight when that doesn't work? Do you tend to freeze, or do you head straight into fight and remain there? For every scenario, you will have a response style and uncovering that pattern can be helpful to your wellbeing and your relationships.

Primitive instincts are deeply rooted and have more of an impact on our day-to-day lives than we may think. They drive us relatively weak mammals to quickly respond to danger, but biologically we have difficulty distinguishing between minor and major life threats (and will always err on the side of caution), which means being stuck in traffic can feel to your body like you are in high jeopardy.

The problem is that the resultant surge in adrenaline, cortisol and other stress chemicals don't get burned off sitting in your car as they would by the flee or fight for survival in the wild.

When the traffic clears and you finally arrive home to find the cat has been sick and there's no milk in the fridge, you are still operating from that previous adrenalised state. This explains why relatively minor annoyances can be the straw that breaks our back, leading to tears at bedtime.

The cumulative effect of many small triggers alongside a few big ones can lead to your alarm dials being turned up too high. This is especially true if your childhood was peppered with real or perceived threats. Often it isn't the event that is the ongoing problem but the meaning you have attached to it and the patterns you have developed to cope with it.

As a child you were programmed to give yourself the best chances of survival emotionally and physically.

You were born believing you mattered and that you would be responded to — the infant drive to cry for attention is testimony to this: a newborn baby *expects* and *demands* to have its needs met *fast*.

In your early years you start to mask your sense of self as you gradually do whatever is required for your human operating system to survive. Who you really are becomes buried as you do your best to keep safe by adapting and reacting to what is going on around you.

The brain will do whatever it can to make sure you survive. Sometimes instead of feeling all the feelings, it will stop you from feeling any feelings. You are left in a state of numb functioning. Ultimately, your brain doesn't care whether you feel or not; it just wants you to keep going.

A two-year-old quickly learns to alter behaviour to get an inattentive caregiver's attention or not trigger an abusive caregiver's temper. A child constantly observes its tribe (parents, siblings, school friends, teachers, coaches, etc) and adapts to fit in or protect itself. This can mean a layering up of the true self and burying of needs, especially if the events that happen are out of your control.

We construct a belief around an event to explain why it is happening: "This has happened to me because I am…. too big, too small, too weak, too selfish", and so on.

As a child you will take all the responsibility for something and draw conclusions, unable to see the full picture. Your desire is to make enough sense of the problem so that you can adapt to cope with it and, better still, reduce the likelihood of it recurring. In a counter-intuitive way, the adaptive behaviour serves a purpose.

The reality is that whilst you are busy navigating and surviving life, many of your basic psychological needs are not met and the body can reflect this. The strategies you used to cope when you were little are not so effective or necessary anymore and they can be causing more harm than good.

This is why we mustn't just treat our behaviours but look to the role, purpose, and function that behaviour is serving in our lives. What did your younger self decide made sense at the time?

As you grow, you start to feel the side effects of your coping strategies. You may have been raised in a somewhat flawed way by caregivers who were trying their best with the skills available to them and who were saddled with their own adaptive behaviours and coping strategies.

Some people have childhoods strewn with trauma and others have largely stable ones with a few issues here and there. Whichever applies to you, it is helpful to check what outdated adaptive behaviours your human operating system is still using.

The truth is life is complicated and no one's childhood was perfect. We grow up operating from a world view because of our experiences.

It takes self-reflection and courage to end repeating cycles of unhelpful or damaging behaviour. Only you can do it, but it's better not to do it alone.

The important thing is to realise that the reason the journey is feeling bumpy is most likely because your younger self is driving the car, and you are in the passenger seat white-knuckling the ride. Don't grab the wheel in a panic! Calmly and kindly switch seats and take over controls.

Internal Family Systems (IFS), founded by Dick Schwartz (ref 11), looks at the different psychological parts that may be playing in your mind's orchestra. His therapeutic system allows you to work out which parts of you are at play and enables you to return as the conductor at your concert.

What might one of your unmet childhood needs have been? What familiar childhood soundtracks are you still playing on repeat? What theories or explanations did you come up with to make sense of your world?

These can often be shaping us in adulthood and discovering them can be the key to unlocking mental and physical pain, worries, unhelpful everyday behaviours, obsessive-compulsive disorder, eating issues and addictions.

You don't have to have had a terrible childhood or major trauma to be running unhelpful programs off these early blueprints. It's the *meaning* your younger self attached to something (that was significant to you at the time) that will be influencing you — more perhaps than the actual event. So don't rule out your past as an influencing factor on your present just because it was relatively straightforward.

Patients often belittle their own situation by comparing it to the friend who has valiantly survived a tragedy. What they are missing is that there isn't a grading system in the brain that says, "This isn't bad enough to be a problem to you". What mattered at the time mattered, and we are interested in what your human operating system has made of it.

We humans like nothing better than a well-trodden path...ah familiarity! The body holds memory in its tissues and the feeling in the body when the smoke alarm is triggered will often be old fears or traumas surfacing even if the event or episode has long passed. This is why in practice we will see patients with a recurrence of an old physical injury that has been retriggered by something minor.

Once the 'negative feeling' has triggered us we need to make sense of it, so the mind uses worry as a means of explanation. It becomes a chicken and egg situation. To assist it in its sense-making exercise (and unfortunately make symptoms more ingrained), the human operating system has the previously mentioned tools of Negative, Familiarity and Confirmation bias at its disposal.

As well as this, our automatic (autonomic in medical speak) nervous system responds to perceived negative stimuli by switching the body's focus from immune response and digestion to pumping our blood around the body faster to the muscles for action and increasing our focus and alertness.

Is it any wonder that prolonged, unprocessed stress stored in the system can lead to recurrent colds, digestive problems, insomnia, immune issues, palpitations, panic attacks, joint pain, migraine, anxiety, anhedonia (lack of joy) and much more?

Your body holds memories of past insults and traumas and is in a constant feedback loop with your mind. Just because you feel a feeling or experience an emotion doesn't mean it is a true reflection of where you are in the present. When you gain perspective over your human operating system and understand that you may be holding unprocessed stress, believing what the voice in your head says and using outdated, false childhood beliefs in adulthood, you can start to help yourself to think and feel better.

7

COVID-19, cancer and other hard times

"You can't tell just by looking at someone what they are dealing with inside."

Danielle Rudd

Illnesses and body changes are frightening and unpredictable — two alarm triggers the human operating system could really do without. It plays to all your primal fears, especially as it can challenge your very survival.

When COVID-19 arrived in 2020, the subsequent chaos turned all our alarm dials up to maximum. Depending on your and your family's mental and physical vulnerability, your poor human operating system went into a degree of brace-brace mode.

Experts were quite rightly worried as they knew COVID had the capacity to seriously disrupt the human body. Think of it as an adaptable computer virus that gets in and messes with the important programmes.

We all felt that something was out to get us. The blaring claxon message was that you needed to isolate yourself from the world and you couldn't even trust your tribe to keep you safe anymore.

Hobbies, movement, exercise, work, and connection all abruptly stopped. Even basic supplies were rationed, and incomes threatened.

Considering our basic human needs and primal survival drivers, it is no wonder that this period in our lives has hangover effects. Depending on your age, stage, and health those effects are still being felt in different ways.

What we see in practice is a range of COVID hangovers from long COVID where the virus has disrupted a person's health by exacerbating a pre-existing condition to COVID-related symptoms such as new debilitating fatigue.

Adolescence and the menopause (both female and male) are also times when our bodies change, and we don't feel our old selves. Random symptoms can develop, and we don't respond to food, exercise, stress, sleep, alcohol, work, etc as we always did. It's like we are navigating a whole new terrain and can feel like our body is somehow failing us and we no longer feel at home.

Hormones are involved in all aspects of our day-to-day lives and so fluctuating levels can lead to an array of symptoms including acne, anxiety, joint pain, lack of self-confidence, insomnia, itching and a change in where our body stores fat. Anything we can do to lower our overall alarm state helps reduce the impact of the hormonal rollercoaster.

Cancer also brings huge fear to us. Abnormal cell growth is happening in our bodies constantly, but it is when our normal hoovering up mechanism is not able to destroy this cell growth that we see disease.

Cancer has a similar picture to COVID in that it feels like a threat, lurking and waiting to get us. It also has long-lasting effects and disrupts our lives. Necessary medical treatments can often be very hard to tolerate, and their side effects bring added symptoms. The resultant picture is of raised alarm in the body.

If you are having cancer treatment — for example chemo, radio, or immunotherapy — your body will be responding to and repairing from each dose. In the weeks and months following it, you can feel extremely fatigued and low. Take comfort in knowing your body is doing what it needs to do to make best use of the treatment.

Having a plan around those days after you have treatment, where you allow yourself enough rest and only do simple tasks such as a gentle walk or reading, allows you to give in to that period of enforced pause so your body can use its energy reserves for healing. Rest is essential to any rehabilitation process.

When patients recover or go into remission, they are often confused that they don't feel elated. They are surprised, baffled, and ashamed that they still 'feel' down. This is completely normal. Think of it as surviving a shipwreck, fighting your way through the stormy sea, and washing up on a seemingly deserted beach. You need time to catch your breath, clean the seaweed and sand off and work out which way is north.

I always advise these patients (and anyone recovering from mental or physical trauma, big or small) to lie on the warm sand and breathe. Don't move a muscle; just lie there and feel the sun's warmth.

Eventually your human operating system will decide it wants to look around and take a wander on this new island. Don't rush it. It knows what it is doing and has an inbuilt compass. When you first sit up and look at the surrounding landscape, you'll start to notice the beach isn't actually deserted but that fellow travellers are also sitting or wandering along it.

Understanding this goes some way to help us cope when we are living alongside or trying to recover from any illness. In my treatments (and any self-help), the focus is on compassionately understanding your thoughts, fears and feelings and reducing the physical build-up of alarm in your body.

Alongside this the aim is to minimise the negative side effects (and optimise the positive effects) of any medical treatment. Overall, we want to harness the body's own return-to-health mechanisms by reducing the alarm state 'obstacle' and emotionally supporting the patient on the journey.

It is important to mention the families and carers of those suffering or who have suffered from illness, trauma, or loss. You are on the same choppy sea, just in a different boat. You have been picking up the pieces, so remember your human operating system has also had its alarm dials turned up and you may well feel worse for a while as your loved one starts to feel better. It may be the first chance you've had to react.

Allow yourself to lie on that beach and numb out. You've been in brace-brace mode in a suspended state of anxiety whilst you have played the support role, and you will take time to adjust.

Sometimes we need to 'wallow' a bit to allow ourselves time to digest our pain and process our feelings. Giving yourself 'hippo time', as Professor Paul McGee (ref 12) describes it, is a necessary part of the recovery process.

Whether you are the patient or the carer, be tender with yourself and seek help to support your mind and body. It's a complex journey you are on/have been on and it is not without side effects.

Health changes and threats and the many messages and effects they bring, challenge our human operating system on a great many levels. It is normal to feel a range of emotions and symptoms and to be dealing with the effects for a long while, even after the threat has passed.

8

Grief and loss

"Grief is not a disease, a disorder or a sign of weakness. It is an emotional, physical and spiritual necessity, the price you pay for love. The only cure for grief is to grieve."

Earl Grollman

Grief is a multifaceted, mercurial beast and navigating it is hard. It shows up differently in each of us; some cry and sob and wear it on their sleeve, but others lock it in a compartment, creating a stable place for it. The latter may not look like they are in grief and often feel shame that they are not 'upset enough'. Does this mean they didn't love the person? Absolutely not.

Grief isn't only a process of the mind. Sometimes the pain is just too much for you to bear and the agony is instead stored in the body. It can present in a myriad of ways such as fatigue, exhaustion, pain, anger, shock, panic, and fear. Dr Judith Joseph (ref 13) describes a state of grief anhedonia that can result when a person is unable to feel any joy.

Someone once described grief to me as a box full of ping pong balls all bouncing around it and causing a spike of pain, loss, and sadness every time they collide.

The only difference with the passing of time is that there are fewer balls in the box and so they crash into each other less frequently, but each collision still triggers the grief spike. It doesn't mean you love the person any less as time goes on, but you are ok for longer periods in between the collisions.

When my father died, I can remember driving back from the hospital in the early hours of the morning literally *consumed with grief.* It was as physical as it was emotional. I was wracked with it.

It was the first time I realised what that phrase really meant and over the following days and weeks, grief would come and *consume* me again and again likes waves crashing over my head and dragging me under water.

Grief isn't only about the loss of a person or a pet. It can be the loss of anything such as an identity, a job, friendship, marriage, a house, or a dream. I have known patients hit grief at a long-awaited retirement, when they don't get the job, or when their child leaves home for university. It's a complex process of letting go of one identity to transform into another and it works at its own pace.

As previously mentioned, we need to allow ourselves time to wallow, digest our pain, process our feelings, and adjust to the new norm.

You can't go under, over or around grief. The only way is through, at your own speed and preferably with some support.

9

Your toolbox

These suggestions all relate to your human operating system's design. The idea is to play to its strengths and natural tendencies: namely that given half the chance, it is always moving towards health and repair but can get stuck in a state of alarm and disorder. We want to move you out of the brace-brace position, calm your system and put it more at ease.

Remember those feel-good chemicals from Chapter 2? The tools in this chapter will help increase your levels of serotonin, dopamine, endorphins and oxytocin in a healthy, sustainable way, creating the right kind of brain cocktail for you to feel better.

Neuroplasticity means your brain is moulded and shaped by what's around you. It takes information in through the senses and adapts to improve your chances — you are wired to survive. Using the tools in this chapter you can steer yourself towards thriving too.

What puts a smile on your face and lifts your spirits? What energises you and unwinds you? What did your younger self love to do? What might you need to *stop* doing in your life? What would you like to *start* doing afresh or *continue* doing? Where do boundaries need to be put in place to give you breathing space?

Self-care requires self-awareness. Take some time to mull it over so that you begin to curate what you need rather than blindly subscribing to the wellness cult that the outside world wants you to join.

If one of your personal values is solitude, that explains why you don't get so much out of that group yoga class. Switching to online sessions may allow you to benefit from the yoga and the alone time, ticking two of your self-care boxes.

Think of the tools below as ways to tweak your wellness dials — to help you to feel better in yourself. In a game of snakes and ladders, these are your ladders, your means of unbracing and self-soothing. You may find that one of these works well for you or a few of them in combination. Many of my patients choose five a day that become as integrated and non-negotiable as brushing their teeth.

It is however important to note that there are times when we are so overwhelmed and exhausted that we can't even consider self-help tools. It's as if we are only succeeding in reaching the surface of the water long enough to gasp a breath before going back under and there is no time for exercise or hobbies. In these moments, reflect on what gives you the best chance of that gulp for air and *ringfence it.*

It might mean crawling into bed in the one hour before your online meeting or parking down the road at school pick-up and listening to your podcast for ten minutes instead of talking at the playground gates.

Do what you need to do until the sea is less choppy and your head is above water. Just do the best you can in the hope that things are going to get better. Your time will come, and this too shall pass.

Prioritise your sleep

You only need to look at pets to realise how important sleep is. They do it all the time! Sleep deprivation raises the body's alarm and is used as a torture tool for a reason. The curious thing about sleep is that when we are tired and consequently, our world looks grey, we cannot believe that a good night's sleep will change anything. It always does.

Alain de Botton (ref 14) suggests that insomnia and forgetfulness are the brain's revenge for not having had breaks in which it can process thoughts and experiences during the day. So don't always fill your time — a car journey without that phone call may offer the mind a chance to daydream and process so that it doesn't have to do so at night.

Your body is a rhythmic machine — in fact all the body systems operate in a rhythm, as does the rest of the natural world — so find your rhythm and stay in it where you can.

Plan your bedtime — if you need to go to sleep at 10.30pm start the process early enough so that you can switch off the light on time. That moment between getting up off the sofa and getting into bed is often filled with another hour's worth of chores, so decide on your 'go to sleep' time and work backwards. This isn't always realistic in our busy lives, but there is usually something that can give to enable you to get to bed earlier.

Get as much morning daylight as you can to maintain a regular circadian rhythm and avoid too much caffeine after midday and close screen use in the evening before bed. Try not to wrap up too warmly, as your body temperature needs to drop to signal the sleep cycle.

When you wake, make it a rule that you at least visit the bathroom, brush your teeth, pull the curtains and make the bed before you look at your phone. This might involve using an old-fashioned alarm clock so that you can plug your phone in across the room (or better still outside the room).

Remember, habits take a while to form and break, so you may need to repeat the good sleep behaviours consecutively before you see results.

Get some rest — stop and be mindful

Rest is different to sleep, rest is resistance to daily life — stopping in the moment. This could mean a bath, shutting your eyes in the waiting room…. just stopping. Put down that phone and unplug from the matrix!

Rest is pausing, rest is grounding. Try lying down flat on your back so that your sensory system is in contact with the bed, floor, sofa, or grass.

The feedback to the brain when we lie down is that we are not under threat because the nervous system knows where it is in space and that its back is covered.

Rest, pause and allow the body and mind to process and regroup, even if it's only for a minute, as without rest, we become overwhelmed and fatigued, and it can all feel too much.

Mindfulness and meditation offer the brain a break. But you don't need to overthink it. Just let your mind drift more often into 'noticing mode' and grab 5– to 10–minute snatches here and there during the day to stare out the window. When you sit and simply observe your breath going in and out, you are exercising parts of your brain that desperately need development. Your mind needs as much nourishment, care and respect as your body. Being internally focused, still and in observation mode instead of externally focused, active and hypervigilant supports your brain and sets it up for resilience.

If in doubt, drink water

Look at what happens to a plant if we don't water it! Our bodies use a lot of water daily and need it for every function, from thinking to filtering toxins. Symptoms such as headaches, stiffness, low mood, and fatigue are often a result of dehydration.

When we become dehydrated, the message to the brain is that there is a problem — those alarm dials get turned up and tension increases. If you feel off-key at all, have a drink of water. It will change your body state for the better, no matter what else is happening.

Magnesium baths

Stress can leach magnesium from your body, and you need magnesium for many things, not least good nervous system function. It is well absorbed through the skin, so a magnesium flakes bath is a great way of ticking one of your wellness boxes. One of the ways low magnesium can show up is in that twitchy eye feeling or tingly fingers and toes.

Move!

Regular exercise is great, but if it's not your bag, just move as often as you can. A dog walk, taking the stairs instead of the lift, dancing round the kitchen or doing squats whilst you wait for the kettle to boil all help to improve blood flow, get oxygen round the body, eliminate waste, and increase the cheerful hormones.

Try to make yourself move every day to remind your body that it isn't an appendage to the desk and that it is capable of other positions. The more you move, the more you will want to move.

It's important to keep muscles strong to support your skeleton, reduce aches and pains, maintain strong bones, and support the organs and circulation. Gentle resistance exercise is a great way to do this and can easily be done at home with weights, in classes or, if you can afford it, with a personal trainer. There are also many free online videos to guide you.

Get out

Numerous studies show that getting outside, in daylight amongst nature, is one of the most effective things we can do to help ourselves feel better. This is especially vital in the darker winter months when daylight is reduced, and the blues can hit.

Listening to birdsong has even outperformed antidepressants in studies on mental wellness as it stimulates the vagus nerve, which mediates our anti-inflammatory and 'rest and digest' system.

Evolutionarily, birds would only chirp when no predators were around, and your primal brain knows this, so stand outside, soak up some Vitamin D, listen to the birds and stare at the horizon to give your vision a break from all that close screen work.

Review your drugs

Make sure you regularly request a 'medications review' to check that any drugs you are taking are necessary and at the correct dosage, that they are not causing side effects through their interactions and there hasn't been a change in usage guidelines. Don't be afraid to use medication, especially to bridge a gap and don't be afraid to question its continued use.

Good vibrations

Music does things to us. You know that song from your teens that transports you to your first kiss at the school disco? The vibration of that music reached your soul and made an imprint. It literally moved you. Listen to your favourite music whenever you can. Make playlists for different moods and moments. Watch things that make you laugh out loud and hang out with people who do the same. Laughter really is medicine for the soul.

Good smells

Make use of the fact that your sense of smell is primal and powerful. Like music it can transport you to a memory in a millisecond. Use essential oils such as peppermint, eucalyptus, and jasmine in your bath, rub them on pulse points, sniff them and be uplifted. Light scented candles. Good smells help settle the alarm state and put us at ease.

Good Grub

As the adage goes, "You are what you eat". So be careful that you are not consuming too many processed foods (PFs) and eating sugars, especially on an empty stomach.

A good rule is that if it has more than a few ingredients, it has most likely been meddled with to an unhealthy extent. Try and apply the 80/20 rule of natural foods/PFs and eat a rainbow of colours and a variety of textures.

We benefit from eating protein, fibre, and natural fats at every meal, especially as we get older. Sugar is to be generally avoided as it causes chemical reactions in the body that are unhelpful on every possible health level. The hunter-gatherer was used to whole, untampered-with foods and periods of feast and famine, not the all-you-can-eat buffet of available foods we have 24 hours a day. Make sure you are not mistaking hunger for thirst, as the brain will sometimes confuse the two.

Stress and weight

When you are stressed, your adrenal glands release adrenaline and cortisol, which changes the way that your body uses sugars, how much energy your muscles burn, and your tolerance to stress. This is a good thing, and we want it to happen when we are wrestling that tiger.

The problem comes when your stress response system gets turned on too frequently and doesn't have time to adequately recover. The constant release of cortisol may increase your risk of developing insulin resistance (which affects how your body deals with sugars), raise your blood sugar, alter your appetite, reduce your ability to burn fat and increase the rate at which you store fat.

If your brain detects through its cortisol sensors that you are under stress or threat, it will assume the worst and that starvation (a major possibility in hunter-gatherer days) is the issue and go into low-power mode. In so doing, it prioritises your energy supply, causing you to store stubborn-to-shift belly fat as a source of energy for you to use in the absence of food.

In most people, this results in weight gain in the abdomen. If you want to lose belly fat, first look at ways of reducing your cortisol levels (by easing your body's overall alarm state using some of these tools) instead of focusing solely on diet. Otherwise, you are fishing bodies out of the water without working out what's pushing them in.

Be useful

I wouldn't have thought my lovely mum had much in common with the ex- bodybuilder, actor, and statesman Arnold Schwarzenegger, but she shares his number one ethos: *be useful*. There is a lot to be said for asking yourself every day how you can add value to something and someone. This ticks so many of the basic human needs, not least to have purpose and meaning, and plays to our primal drive to be part of something. This raises our 'virtue status', which pleases the primal brain.

Subtract

Culture is always telling us to add more to our lives, but *subtracting* something can also be helpful. Clearing out a cupboard so that you have fewer pans to fight with, cancelling a diary date and letting that dysfunctional relationship go can free up mental and physical room and help you to either welcome something or someone better in or just bask in the pleasure of the space. Where can you push back against the demands of life by saying no and clearing?

Clean up your screen and make it grey

Watch out for signs that your social media and TV diet is poor. Remember those algorithms are going to give you more of what you engage with, so follow uplifting, funny, and heartwarming sites as opposed to those which enrage and alarm you. It's like a menu in a restaurant — be careful what you are ordering every day. If it makes you feel low to see that beautiful friend showing off about her holiday/car/partner, then mute her. Social media platforms are highly curated and unfortunately, they feed every human operating system fear. You don't necessarily have to unfollow someone, but muting them gives you a break from the feeling of their perceived 'higher status' being rubbed in your face.

A quick five-minute scroll that becomes half an hour before dropping off to sleep can leave us feeling inadequate, lonely, and hopeless, and that becomes the unconscious setting for your brain at night. It's not that you are being weak. It's that the technology is designed to overcome normal attention-stopping cues and hold your focus. It is no coincidence that the dopamine hit your brain gets from scrolling is very hard to resist. It is also no coincidence (or surprise) that many of the tech titans have publicly stated that they do not allow their own children to freely use the very tech they sell.

Switching your screen to 'greyscale' is a way of making the images less attractive to your dopamine-craving brain. Even if you only switch to greyscale in the evenings, this may well help to reduce the mindless scrolling that snatches your precious time (and leaves you feeling strangely overcooked and dissatisfied).

Take a breath

If you are shocked, you immediately take a sharp breath and raise your chest and shoulders. The message from your body to your mind is that there is a clear and present danger. The mind then signals for all the high alerts to switch on and the alarm dials get turned up. To reverse this, we need to do the opposite style of breathing which will turn those unhelpful dials back down.

Sit, stand, or lie and with your mouth shut take a full nose 'in-breath' — pushing out your tummy to create a pot belly. Breathing from the diaphragm in this way sends all the right signals to the brain that confirm you are safe and leads it towards rest and digest mode. As you get to the top point of your in-breath, do a short sharp extra breath before breathing out (with mouth shut) through your nose. This is called the physiological sigh. Repeat this for a few breaths and you will have signalled to your primal brain that those alarm dials can turn down a bit.

There are lots of great breathing apps online that will suggest breathing exercises with timings. One way is to breathe in for two seconds, hold for three and out for four. It doesn't matter what timings you use, just make sure you breathe out for longer than you breathe in, it feels comfortable to you and doesn't feel strained. It might make you yawn, which is a sign that your nervous system is calming down and your human operating system is smiling inside.

Stretch it out

Before you get into bed at night and first thing in the morning try stretching your body into the *reverse* position of your everyday life. For example, stand in the corner of your room and put your hands on each wall, slowly leaning forwards — this opens the chest and shoulders, *reversing* the computer/driving/desk hunch.

You can do the same thing for other areas of your body (you simply need to think of the opposite direction to your habitual postures). You can lie on a rolled-up towel or roller to enhance the stretch and release tension.

Yoga, Pilates or Qigong (either online or in a class) are a useful combination of stretch, strength, balance and breathing.

Get a hobby

Hobbies are brilliant for ticking so many of our basic human needs: sense of belonging, mindfulness, pleasure, meaning, self-agency and purpose, to name a few. It is often in a hobby that you can find your tribe. I'm always interested in asking my patients what their hobbies are, what communities they are part of and what this brings to their lives. The answer is *a great deal*. It's useful to remember back to what you were interested in as a child (before life and other people's opinions got in the way) and investigate hobbies linked to that.

Scan yourself

When you are lying down on the sofa or bed, imagine you have a scanner running up and down your body, checking for where the tension or alarm is showing up. Where is the alarm stored? Where does the scanner beep?

Your human operating system will have stored its stress somewhere and by finding and acknowledging this, your body and mind can often deal with it better. It's like a messy file that's been left by the office water cooler, cluttering up the place. The human operating system likes nothing more than knowing that a file has been first located (it always knew that a file was mislaid) and placed in the right cabinet or shredded (aah, nice and neat!).

This body scan can also help you to identify where you are holding physical tension — your neck? Your jaw? This means you can make a more informed choice regarding any treatment you have or which tool you need from the toolbox.

Hello toes, hello nose

Lie down on a comfy surface and start at your toes, squeezing and releasing them before slowly moving to your feet, ankles, calves, knees, thighs and upwards to the top of your head. In your mind, name each part and enjoy the sense of calm in the body when you reach the end. This naming and sensing of all body areas is reassuring to the primal brain and once again has the effect of reducing your stress state, which will make you feel better.

Splash yourself

If you are feeling stressed or anxious, run your

wrists under cold water or splash your face with cold water to help reset the system and reduce the alarm state. This directly impacts the nervous system, acting as a trip switch.

What soothes you?

Stop and consider what you like to do and what is restorative to you. We can get caught up in the social norms or coffee with friends, exercise classes, manicures, the pub, golf, and shopping when what truly soothes and restores us is time alone, sorting through photos or reading a book.

Be mindful of who and what you give your precious spare time to. Saying no in the moment can be hard, so buy yourself time when asked to do something by saying you'll check your personal/family/work diary and get back to someone.

This means you can ask yourself if you really want to make that date or would prefer to curl up with the dog and watch that documentary. Your time is of value — don't waste it.

Get it out of your head

Persistent thoughts, worries, and the 'stuff you wish you had or hadn't said' can run in a loop around your mind, cluttering up the system and perpetuating old, unhelpful stories and beliefs.

Writing them down or saying them out loud is extremely helpful to our human operating system and can help you tune into your intuition and gut feel, which is especially helpful when making important decisions or trying to process an issue or event. You don't always need the workings of your brain to be heard by a person — the rear-view mirror or a piece of paper can be a great depositing ground. It's amazing how good it can feel to just get it out. For your brain, it's as if you have finally done the filing and your system can breathe a sigh of relief and move on to wherever is next.

Remember to burn the piece of paper afterwards so that no one reads it or keep your journal somewhere safe and private. Cars are brilliant at keeping secrets.

Hang on in there — it's not wrong, it's new

Change can lead to a feeling of being afloat in unchartered waters. The human operating system doesn't like this — it's unfamiliar, for starters! Be careful however not to confuse something unfamiliar with it being wrong.

Your brain is a fan of what is recognisable and routine, so remember that when you change a habit or try something new, it will take a while (often 21 days) for your system to accept it and for its benefits to show.

Promise yourself you will review how you feel after a set period, as you need to develop the metaphoric and literal muscle memory for the new thing to get established so the subconscious can allow it to be part of your repertoire.

Be less Solomon

Have you heard of the Solomon Paradox? According to the story, King Solomon was known for giving great advice. To his subjects he was extremely wise, and they turned to him in times of trouble. His personal life however was a mess. He couldn't apply the same rational logic to his own problems and instead made disastrous emotion-based decisions.

We are better at solving other people's problems than our own because we think more clearly when we are not involved in the problem. Our emotional brain takes a back seat and lets our rational brain lead.

When faced with a difficult situation or decision, avoid getting caught in the Solomon Paradox by zooming out from yourself and hovering above the problem — as if you were discussing an issue that belongs to your friend.

Sometimes, writing the situation out and making

a pros and cons list can give you the initial *emotional separation* from the issue to help you fight back against this powerful paradox.

Chunk by chunk

My big sister is epic. One of her many skills is problem-solving. People turn to her as a sounding board because she is kind, compassionate, enthusiastic, and optimistic — there are very few conundrums she doesn't find a solution for. This is fundamentally because she believes in the 'chunk by chunk' approach. Feel overwhelmed? Break it down and tackle it one bite at a time. Just take each next right step to make things feel more manageable and remember, as the philosopher Seneca said, 'luck is often where preparation meets opportunity', so keep chipping away in the direction of your dream, and you'll be ready when luck gives you a leg up.

Learn to trust calm

We don't always know what's good for us. This is because our past memory of it in a different guise may have meant it wasn't all it was cracked up to be.

For example, if you grew up in an intermittently volatile home, there would have been periods of calm in between the chaos.

During these periods of calm, you would have learnt to anticipate the next traumatic episode, so the calm times just felt like waiting for the other shoe to drop. You might have become a busy bee, always on the go, which means that when you start to try meditation or rest, it can feel wrong and even unsafe until your human operating system learns it is ok. Stick with it and go gently. Try it in small doses until you rewire.

Forgive or repair for your own sake

Holding on to blame and resentment ends up poisoning the victim. The feelings must go somewhere, and they usually get stored in the body, showing up in a myriad of symptoms. The cultural message of forgiveness is that we should accept what 'we' or 'they' did when, really, the peace that comes from forgiving is gained from the perspective of understanding how and why something happened.

It's the difference between standing with your nose pressed up against that blur of colour and texture or stepping back far enough to see the painting.

An alcoholic parent abusing their child isn't right or acceptable, but understanding through an historical perspective that they were similarly abused by their parent and carried the resultant trauma scars and lack of skills forward allows you to give yourself the grace that you were most likely collateral damage in someone else's story rather than their target.

You can't change what happened, but you can choose to curiously look at what came before and after it — what surrounded it from both parties' perspectives — and from that, you make some sense of the story and release your system from the burden of being stuck in the past. There may always be grief to navigate, but forgiveness allows you to move forward for your own sake.

The same can be applied to the first step towards repair, which can be what it takes to eventually mend a fractured relationship. Holding out the olive branch is a hard thing to do at times and doesn't always result in a relationship healing because sometimes the damage has gone too far. However, leaning into reconciliation brings a semblance of calm to a situation and turns the heat down, which paves the way for a more harmonious future for both parties involved. Unequivocally owning our side of the problem, admitting and accepting it, is always a positive move. It's a step towards peace.

Value tag what you want

Selective filtering, selective attention and value

tagging are all brain tools for making sure that in the wild, you focused on what was important, ignored distractions and were emotionally driven to fight for what you needed.

The brain finds it very hard to distinguish what is real and what isn't, so use vision boards, pictures of your dreams stuck on the fridge door or mirror and any other simulation to make your dream familiar to your brain and help to reduce roadblocks to change.

Remember that uncertainty and novelty are the biggest threats to the brain, and it will *avoid loss* more than it will chase reward. Embody and visualise the thing that you want so that it is a part of your everyday sensory life.

Make use of these primal tendencies if you are trying to manifest or create anything by priming your brain to notice and grasp opportunities that bring you closer to what you want.

Give yourself (and others) a High 5

In the words of motivational speaker Mel Robbins, give yourself a high-5 in the mirror every morning. This might seem cheesy, but research shows that a high-5 positively changes both your chemistry and your mindset. There's a reason why the NBA and other sports teams high-5 each other before heading into a game. Every time you high-5, you communicate a mood boosting mix of acknowledgement, belief, celebration and encouragement alongside a shot of feel-good dopamine and oxytocin. Matching physical motion (that is unexpected to the brain) with a positive thought is the fastest way to create a new neural pathway. The Motivational Power of a High-5 research study showed that over three groups of students, those who were only high-fived before a test outperformed those who were given verbal encouragement and praise for their ability, effort and perseverance. A high-5 to yourself in the mirror every morning, regardless of how rubbish you may be feeling, boosts your system and fulfills your emotional need to be seen, encouraged and believed in.

10

Recap

"Self-awareness is our capacity to stand apart from ourselves and examine our thinking, our motives, our history, our scripts, our actions, and our habits and tendencies."

Stephen R Covey

The world has changed a great deal, but we haven't. We are still using the same strategies and running the same hard drive as we did when hunting down supper and sheltering from the elements on the African plains and there is a reason for this — it works.

We have an amazing design with an inbuilt intelligence that steers us away from danger and towards safety. We've got several tricks up our human sleeve to alert us to and turn us away from trouble, and if these fail, we have many more ways to ride out the problem and cope. Our drive to survive will make us behave in certain predictable ways.

Our wellbeing depends on keeping our body's chemistry in balance. This balance is always being challenged in the modern world (think social media scrolling) as it can be easily manipulated and disrupted.

We are a tribal lot and being connected to each other emotionally and physically is essential to our wellbeing, which is why relationships affect us so deeply. We are acutely aware of and affected by dissonance. We like to get along, feel needed, and have a purpose, and we employ the tactics of copying, flattering, and conforming to help us achieve this.

Status really matters to us, and we are hard-wired through our brain's status detection system to monitor our own and others' positions when it comes to status games such as virtue, wealth, strength, appearance, power, and popularity.

Our bodies are constantly working towards health and when we remove obstacles, our wellbeing flows. This is often easier said than done, as the pressures of modern living don't always facilitate good lifestyle habits.

The answer is to steer yourself *gradually* towards a healthier path even if you can't make leaps and bounds. One walk per week is a hundred per cent more than no walks per week.

An undeniable truth is that time passes faster than you think and soon you will have made many of those small steps in the more favourable direction and a good habit will have formed. Another truth is that sometimes it only takes one positive move to motivate you towards another. Pick one good thing for your mind and body and ringfence it from the rest of life's demands. Your human self deserves it.

On occasion when I have read self-help books, I have felt worse because all the advice makes sense, but I have no energy left to implement it! In fact, on those days, I have barely enough energy left to brush my teeth before bed.

If this is you,

a) you are not alone

b) it will get better, and

c) prioritise rest where possible.

You are most likely somewhat overwhelmed and exhausted. If you were lost in the middle of a forest in a storm and your iPhone had 8% battery you wouldn't try and stream a movie. Be kind to yourself, take any help you can get and be reassured that even in this depleted state, your inbuilt healing compass will be steering you towards feeling better.

It may not always look and feel that way, and things may get worse before you improve, but trust in your human design. It's got an excellent track record.

We are all on the sea bobbing about on different boats, but for some, the waters are choppier than others and the boat less robust. I hope this book helps you to understand your human design and your unique version of it a little better as you reflect on your own story. Most of all, I hope it helps you to be kinder to yourself.

In a world that often feels out of control and in a body that doesn't come with a manual, it is helpful to grasp the basics of our makeup so that we can feel a sense of self-authority and self-agency. Being conscious of our inner voice, our behaviours, body responses and learned patterns is the first step in improving our overall sense of wellbeing. It means we can help ourselves and help others.

My intention with this book has been to give you a realistic look at how to cope better and take back some control of your reactions and responses to the circumstances in which you find yourself.

Your conscious mind has learnt a lot. It now understands and can make more sense of its subconscious primal wiring. It's early days; go easy on yourself and repeat the good stuff until it sticks. Keep this book to hand so that you can dip in and out of the relevant chapters when you need a reminder.

Remember that the first step is to have the knowledge so that you can start to manage your wiring better. Keep reminding yourself that you are human and running a hard drive that needs tuning and maintenance to function better in its modern surroundings.

We humans are a big deal. We've come a long way, and we are survivors. The best way we can thrive as well as survive is to know ourselves, remember we matter and make others feel they do too.

Of all the things I have learnt over my years as a practitioner the human's need to matter stands above all others. I think it's because if you matter you are significant, needed, wanted, listened to, heard, missed, and ultimately **safe**.

It's what we all want and it's because we're
human.

References

1. Glennon Doyle, Abby Wambach, Amanda Doyle — wecandohardthingspodcast.com

2. Bessel Van Der Kolk — besselvanderkolk.com

3. Andrew Huberman — hubermanlab.com

4. Edward Tufte — edwardtufte.com

5. Tristan Harris — thesocialdilemma.com

6. Richard Wilkins — theministryofinspiration.com

7. Liz Ivory — theministryofinspiration.com

8. Tom Palmer — tomgpalmer.com

9. Jon Kabat-Zinn — jonkabat-zinn.com

10. Morgan Housel — morganhousel.com

11. Dick Schwartz — Internal Family Systems (IFS) — ifs-institute.com

12. Professor Paul McGee — thesumoguy.com

13. Dr Judith Joseph — drjudithjoseph.com

14. Alain de Botton — alaindebotton.com

Further reading

Dr Anders Hansen — drandershansen.com

Dr Brené Brown — brenebrown.com

Dr Alok Kanojia — healthygamer.gg

Dr Becky Kennedy — goodinside.com

Dr Bruce Lipton — brucelipton.com

Dr Howard Schubiner — unlearnyourpain.com

Dr Judith Joseph — drjudithjoseph.com

Dr Martha Beck — marthabeck.com

Dr Mary Claire Haver — maryclairewellness.com

Dr Pooja Lakshmin — poojalakshmin.com

Dr Rangan Chatterjee — drchatterjee.com

Dr Russell Kennedy — theanxietymd.com

Dr Tara Swart — taraswart.com

Elizabeth Day — elizabethday.org

Emma Reed Turrell — emmareedturrell.com

James Clear — jamesclear.com

Johann Hari — johannhari.com

Mel Robbins — melrobbins.com

Mo Gawdat — mogawdat.com

Steven Pinker — stevenpinker.com

T J Power — tjpower.co.uk

Will Storr — thescienceofstorytelling.com

humanprogress.org

Dr Michael Rich — digitalwellnesslab.org

Steven Bartlett — stevenbartlett.com

Dr Gabor Mate — drgabormate.com

Dr Kristin Neff — selfcompassion.org

Dr Christine Bishara — fromwithinmedical.com

Damian Hughes and Jake Humphrey — thehighperformancepodcast.com

Dan Siegel — drdansiegel.com

Acknowledgements

As a child, I loved writing.

Copious poems, stories, essays and love notes were bestowed upon my parents, who treated me as if I were a celebrated, acclaimed author, giving me confidence and courage right from the start. It's thanks to them that I had the self-belief to become an osteopath and coach, run my own practice, and now write this book. They set me up for success.

I started talking about *Why do I feel like this?* to my dear friend and talented writer **Rachel Johnson** a long time ago. Thanks Rach, for encouraging me to give it a go.

Many people were kind enough to discuss ideas or be guinea pig readers:

Thank you to **Kari Ambrose, Carolyn Askar, Emma Askar, Huly Askar, Helena Aston, Carl Bianco, Paula Blacker, Joseph Borlase, Barney Brown, Joanna Brown, Lucy Brittain, Laura Burdess, Sheila Bury,**

Barbara Carr, Annie Caldeira, Ethan Caldeira, Sophie Clarkin, Alex Clementson, Andrew Clementson, Josh Clementson, Max Clementson, Sam Coppinger, Kathryn Dean, Nicky Dibbo, Brigitte Dowsett, Leanne

Duffield, Tray Durrant, Emma Elliott, Peter Elliott, Gaynor Farrer-Brown, Charlie Fawkner Corbett,

Mike Fawkner Corbett, Jan Galland, Anna Goodall, Hannah Golding, Shannon Goree, Emma Haxton, Mick Hext, Amelia Hodgetts, Sophie Hogan, Hen Horton,

Kate Hudson, Simon Hudson, Sarah Hydes, Emma Kew,

Floss Lee, Julie Lewers,

Phillipa Marshall, Gavin Matthews, Maddie McCarthy, Rosemary McClatchey, Gaye McKeogh, Alizee Middleton, Kate Moir, Sue Morris, Sarah Mosely, Meri Mower, Joy Murphy, James Murray, Zoe Myatt, Alan Myatt,

Nicky Neill, Charlotte Nicholl, Natalie Noakes, Amanda Page, Sophie Parkes, Sam Pemberton, Lucy Phillips, Sarah Powell, Camilla Quesnel, Shana Ray, Nina Revell, Nicky Sanderson, Emma Shah, Sanjeev Shah,

Jemima Small, Nicola Small, Kate Spark, Tilly Spark, Jono Stebbings, Lisa Stebbings, Lizzie Symons,

Polly Swann, Sandra Tearney, Esther Ter Haar, Caroline Tonder, Hannah Tonder,

Geoff Tresman, Sue Tresman, Alex Tucker, Julia Tuhill, Janet Thirkettle, Deidre Van Der

Waag, Tilly Wallace, Bryony Warren, Andy Wells,

Charles Tyzack, Krisztina Tyzack, Kathy Aitchison, Darryl Sowden, Polly Leach, Susanna Knox, Tilly Armitage Beazeley, Kate Gethin, Claire Howard, Lorraine Hutchison,

Eliis McCarthy, Abi Evans, Nikki Evans,

Fi Warren-Smith, Alex Whittenbury, Katie Wiggin, Gill Williamson, Sandra Wilkinson, and Gilly Woodhouse for putting up with my book chat over the years and giving me such valuable feedback. Your enthusiasm and faith spurred me on.

Thanks to my wonderful Orchard Clinic dream team of Sally Knight, Julia Deacon, Lisa Harris, Ali Lawrance, Tom Morgan, Sam Strudley, Carrie Schmidt, Georgia Turner, Amanda Watt, Jayne Wells, Abi Williamson and Cass Clayton who are a joy to work with and teach me so much.

Thank you to Richard Wilkins and Liz Ivory for running the courses that enabled me to fully understand what damage that negative voice in my head was doing and learn to separate from it. You are two amazing and generous people and I highly recommend your life-changing courses.

Thank you to my editor Michelle Emerson, who is patient, wise and talented. I knew you were the one for me when your dogs joined in on our first conversation. You have been exactly who I needed to get this book published.

Also, thanks to my illustrator **Ian Ward,** who drew the wonderful images at the start of each chapter and took the time to really understand what I wanted. He also had the good grace not to laugh at my amateur sketches!

Thank you to social media guru **Tilly Wallace** — linkedin.com/in/tilly-wallace-48549a1aa and web designer **Alex Le Grand** — legrandsolutions.co.uk and **Hazel Eastlake** at petitedigital.co.uk for all their help and support.

Huge thanks to the talented **Fin Wells** — Narcova_ for his help (and patience) with the audible recording. Fin, you are not only a brilliant photographer, musician and songwriter but also a tech wizard.

Thank you to **Carrie Schmidt** for being there since we were small and for being my constant companion through life. You are an amazing person and friend, and I am so lucky to also work with you. I never take for granted that we share so much history. It is a gift to be known so well.

When asked for her best writing tip, prolific author Kristin Hannah advises to surround yourself with the smartest people you can and listen to them. So, I did. Thank you, **Jane Hext**, for being what I can only describe as a marvel. You were generous with both your time and expertise, and I will always look back on our afternoons of (strong) tea, biscuits and the whiteboard with fondness. Your fabulous combination of constructive criticism and humour was exactly the kind of help I needed. My only regret in finishing this book is that our meetings have ended. Please can I book you for the next one?

Jayne Wells, you have been my soulmate, colleague, ally, supporter and partner in crime for 18 years. You are the best antidote for the negative voice in my head and I can't thank you enough for all you have done to help me write this book. Thank you for buying me late-night post-course whiskies in motorway hotel bars, always having my back, making me laugh and listening to me witter on. You truly are my angel and I love working alongside you.

Tim John, thank you for trusting me to work in your practice early on in my career and for our epic London lunches. You are a fabulous role model not just as an osteopath but also in the way you employ so many wellness tools in your life. You walk the walk as well as talk the talk, and it is no wonder that you are adored by your patients. You were the perfect person to ask to write the foreword for this book.

Thanks to my patients over the years who have trusted me to take care of them and shared their lives with me. I am blessed to be your osteopath and have learnt so much from you all.

Thank you to my family; to my sister **Cory,** who has always made me feel so loved, told me I can do whatever I want to do, believed in me and stood by my side on the journey – I love you so much. **Ash**, **Maddie** and **Charlie,** thank you for all your love and support.

Thank you to my mother-in-law **Lena,** who (alongside my late father-in-law **Paul**) has always been my champion and friend. She has loved me like a daughter and makes the best chicken pie I have ever tasted.

My **dad, Brian**, passed away just before COVID-19. He would have absolutely loved me publishing this book and was a firm believer in giving anything a go. Dad, you instilled in me a sense of self-worth that I am forever grateful for. My grief for you still comes and slaps me around the face on a regular basis. You mattered so much and are very much missed.

So many thanks go to my **mum**, **Sally**, who is the best in the business. She not only encouraged me to write this book but did endless jobs in the background to enable me to sit down in front of the screen. I feel so lucky to work alongside you, Mum, you are so dedicated to us all and to The Orchard Clinic and I am blessed that you are always interested and enthusiastic about my life.

You embody generosity of spirit and Dad would be so proud of how you carry on. I love you with all my heart.

And lastly, my own little tribe:

Rocco the dog, my constant late-night writing companion. His gentle snoring has been a comfort and a distraction in equal measure. He thinks whatever I do is great and who doesn't need that in their life?

Ben, thank you for our late-night chats and for being so kind and funny. You will never know how much I love spending time with you and how I have always cherished our car journeys together. Your thesaurus-like ability to come up with the right word for one of this book's chapters, make tea and toasties at midnight, massage my shoulders *and* listen to your podcast all at the same time is unrivalled. You are my champ.

G, you are the best company and I love our trips together. Thank you for your unwavering support, belief in me and no-nonsense approach to my book wobbles. Your perfectly timed turns of phrase are second to none and you always encouraged me to keep going at just the right moment. Your funny, loving Snap messages and assumption that I would get this book written meant more than you know. You're my queen.

And lastly to **Dom**. Thank you for giving me the

space to write. Not easy at this busy stage of life in this busy cave of ours. You have been so patient, encouraging and, as ever, by my side, believing in me. Those cups of tea placed next to my laptop and kind critique of my grammar have made all the difference. I know my ongoing battle with commas has broken you at times! Thank you for all you do for our little unit and for being the person I get to be human with – I simply adore you.

Author bio

Kelley Waters graduated in 1999 and has provided over 30,000 treatments in her 25-year career as an osteopath and wellbeing coach. She has always been curious about behaviour, people's stories, the awesome design of the body and how we humans navigate our world.

Kelley runs a busy multi-disciplinary health practice in Berkshire where she also lives with her husband Dom, son Ben, daughter G, two cats, and a very *human* dog.

She hopes that this book gives you a sense of the therapeutic encounter of her treatment room and that it will sit on your nightstand as a comforting resource to help you and your own tribe feel better.

For more information or to contact Kelley go to:
- whydoifeellikethis.co.uk
- kelleywaters.com
- theorchardclinic.co.uk

and to follow her on Instagram:
- why_doifeellikethis
- the_orchardclinic

Scan the QR code to get straight to my website.